The Soccer Math Book
The Rematch!

Adrian Lobley

For Sebastian

Books by Adrian Lobley

<u>*Learning Math*</u>
The Soccer Math Book (Ages 4-6)
The Soccer Math Book - The Re-match! (Ages 5-7)
The Soccer Math Book - The Christmas Match (Ages 6-8)
The Soccer Math Book - The Birthday Party (Ages 7-8)
The Soccer Math Book - The World Cup (Age 9)

<u>*Learning to Read*</u>
A Learn to Read Book: The Football Match (Ages 4-5)
A Learn to Read Book: The Tennis Match (Ages 4-5)

<u>*Historical Fiction*</u>
Kane and the Mystery of the Missing World Cup (Ages 7-10)
Kane and the Christmas Football Adventure (Ages 7-10)

<u>*Humor*</u>
The Ridiculous Adventures of Sidebottom and McPlop (Ages 7-10)
The Footballing Adventures of Sidebottom and McPlop (Ages 8-11)

For more info go to: www.adrianlobley.com

With thanks to:

Sebastian Wraith-Lobley, Sarah Wraith, Nick Callaghan, Lewis Coates
Callan Nicholson, Asher Nicholson, Miss Pugh, Christopher Chamberlain
Finlay Cronshaw, Fin Goodall, Paul Goodall

Front/back cover illustrations by:
Alyssa Josue

At the beginning of a match the coach decides the positions where the players should play. This is called the team's **formation**.

Carry out the following steps…
- Find player number 4 in the diagram below.
- Now draw a straight line from player 4 to player 7.
- Then draw a straight line from player 7 to player 8.
- Then draw a straight line from player 8 to player 11.
- Finally draw a straight line from player 11 to player 4.

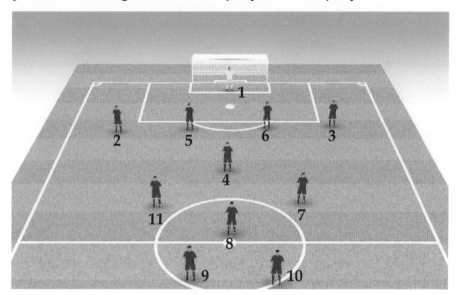

Is the shape of these 4 midfielders a circle, diamond or a triangle?
Write the word in the sentence below…

The team is playing in a _____ formation.

If you answered the question correctly then enter a score of 1-0 here:

In top soccer matches there are the following number of match officials:

- One 'Referee'

- Two 'Assistant Referees'

'Assistant Referees' used to be called 'Linesmen' and 'Lineswomen'

- One 'Fourth Official'

A 'Fourth Official' is a 'spare' referee in case the actual referee gets injured. He also has tasks to do.

How many officials are there in total? ☐

Number line

0   1   2   3   4   5   6   7   8   9   10

Enter 1-0 here if you got the answer correct. ☐ — ☐

Look at one of the **black** shapes on the soccer ball below. How many sides does the black shape have?

If a shape has 4 sides it is a square. If a shape has 5 sides it is a pentagon.

Is the shape a square or a pentagon?

Look at one of the **white** shapes on the soccer ball below. How many sides does the white shape have?

If a shape has 5 sides it is a pentagon. If a shape has 6 sides it is a hexagon.

Is the white shape a pentagon or a hexagon?

Enter the number you got correct in the first box and the number wrong in the second box.

To score a goal you have to draw a route to goal which is made up from **even** numbers. You can only go vertically or horizontally, not diagonally.

Starting at the bottom of the number grid below, can you find the route (it has been started for you)?

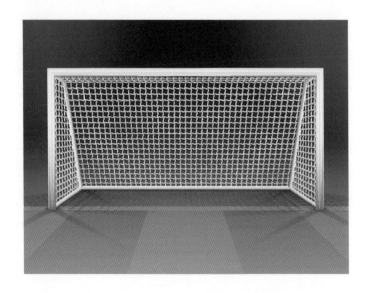

4	3	9	3	1
2	9	4	8	2
2	6	8	5	6
3	5	3	9	4
7	9	2	1	6

Enter 1-0 if you got it correct, or 0-1 if you didn't: ☐ — ☐

To score a goal you have to draw a route to goal which is made up from **odd** numbers. You can only go vertically or horizontally, not diagonally.

Starting at the bottom of the number grid below, can you find the route?

4	7	8	8	1
3	9	4	8	2
9	6	9	5	7
3	5	3	4	5
8	2	2	3	1

Enter 1-0 if you got it correct, or 0-1 if you didn't:

In professional soccer a team consists of 11 players plus another 7 substitutes sitting on the bench.

First Team

Substitutes

How many players are there in total? ☐

Of the 7 substitutes, the coach can bring a maximum of 3 of them on in a match.

Substitutes

If the coach does make 3 substitutions, how many substitutes does that leave who do not get to play? ☐

Enter your score for this page: ☐ — ☐

How many black studs does the soccer boot below have?

As there are always 2 boots, how many studs are on the other boot?

To work out how many studs there are in total on both boots complete the following sum:

$$\begin{array}{r} 12 \\ + \ 12 \\ \hline \\ \hline \end{array}$$

Add the numbers downwards, starting with the ones nearest me, below the blue arrow

Enter your score for this page:

At half-time in a soccer match, players are given oranges to provide them with energy. The coach has cut the orange below into 2 pieces.

He has now given you 1 of the pieces.

As you have 1 of the 2 pieces. We write that as: ½. This is called a half. So you have ½ an orange. Writing it like this (½), is called a **fraction**.

The coach cuts his next orange into 4 pieces.

You are given 1 piece out of the 4. This is called a quarter of the orange.

Draw a circle around the fraction below that is the same as a quarter.

½   ¼

Enter your score for this page: ☐ — ☐

To find out the **multiples** of the number 3, keep adding 3. So it's...3, 6, 9, 12, 15, 18...

Would you like to score a goal for your team?

Draw a route to goal from **multiples of 3**, ie the numbers above.

4	13	19	8	15
6	9	15	18	12
9	4	9	3	7
12	3	13	8	5
8	6	2	6	20

Enter 1-0 if you got it correct, or 0-1 if you didn't:

9

Read out the score below.   Then read out the goalscorers.

Result	City's Goalscorers
Atlanta 6 - 0 Portland	Sebastian 3, Jane 2, Sophia

There is a '3' next to Sebastian's name above, which means Sebastian scored 3 of City's 6 goals.   Jane has scored 2.

If a player's name appears as a goalscorer but it has no number by his name, he has scored 1 goal. So above, Sophia has scored 1 goal.

A player who scores 3 or more goals in a match has scored a hat-trick

Below is the next match result:

Result	City's Goalscorers
New York 7 – 1 Columbus	Mia 3, Emily 3, Jake

How many players scored a hat-trick in this match? ☐

How many goals did Jake score? ☐

Enter your score for this page: ☐ — ☐

What is Portland's **Goal Difference** in the 4 matches below? The first one has been done for you…

The number of goals a team scores minus the number they concede gives their **Goal Difference**

Result			Goal Difference
Portland	4-1	New York	+3
Portland	3-1	Houston	☐
Portland	3-2	Seattle	☐
Portland	0-0	Chicago	☐

If a team have scored more goals than they have conceded, a '+' (plus) sign is put in front of the number

Now use the number line below to help you work out what Portland's **Goal Difference** is over the 4 games. In other words, what is the answer to this sum: 3 + 2 + 1 + 0 = ☐

Number Line

0   1   2   3   4   5   6   7   8   9   10

Enter your score for this page: ☐ — ☐

To help you with this game, fill in the boxes below with **multiples of 4**. To do this, add 4 each time. The first 2 numbers have been completed for you.

4	8				

The opposition team have been given a penalty kick! Use the clues below to work out which square the opposition attacker kicks the ball towards.

Cross out the numbers in the picture, after answering each clue:

- He **doesn't** shoot at any of the odd numbers
- He **doesn't** shoot at any number less than 3
- He **doesn't** shoot at any number that is a multiple of 4

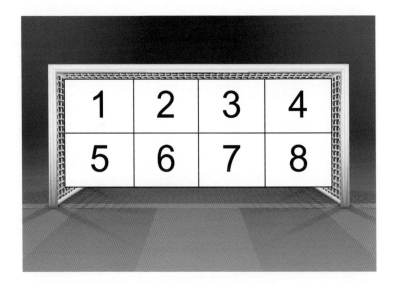

Enter the number of the square where the opposition attacker shoots

Enter your score for this page: ☐ — ☐

It's a penalty kick shoot out!

You have to take 5 penalty kicks. Look at the goal below and cross out 5 different numbers where you would like your shots to go.

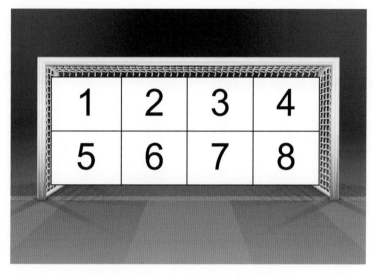

If any number you chose is an even number, check this box

If any number is a multiple of 3 then check this box

If any number is a multiple of 4 then check this box

If any number is greater (ie bigger) than 6 then check this box

If any number is less than 3 then check this box

Now count up the number of boxes you checked. This is the number of penalty kicks you scored. Enter this number in the box below so see what the penalty shoot out score was between your team and the opposition. Did you win?

Penalty Kick Shoot-Out score (out of 5) : ☐ — 3

The opposition team have been given another penalty kick! Use the clues below to work out which square the opposition striker kicks the ball towards.

Cross out the numbers in the picture, after answering each clue:

- He **doesn't** shoot at any square that is a multiple of 3
- He **doesn't** shoot at any number that has 2 digits in it
- He **doesn't** shoot at any even numbers
- He **doesn't** shoot at any number below 6

Enter the number of the square where the opposition attacker shoots

Enter your score for this page: ☐ — ☐

Below is a league table with 4 teams in it. The teams are in blue.

Team	Played	Won	Drawn	Lost
Portland	2	2	0	0
Atlanta	2	1	1	0
New York	2	0	1	1
Columbus	2	0	0	

Each team has **played** the same number of games so far. Can you spot how many matches each team has **played**? ☐

Find Portland in the table. Now look along that row.
How many matches have Portland **won**? ☐

Columbus have **played** 2 matches. In the table you can see they have not **won** either match and they have not tied (**drawn**) either match. So how many matches have they **lost**?   Enter the number in the table.

Enter your score for this page: ☐ — ☐

If you add the number of games a team has **won**, tied(**drawn)** and **lost** it equals the number of matches they have **played**.

The person writing the league table below has missed out two of the numbers by mistake!

Help him by working out what the missing numbers are and writing them in.

Team	Played	Won	Drawn	Lost
Chicago	2	2	0	0
Houston	2	1	0	
Dallas	2	1	0	1
Miami	2		0	2

He's missed out two numbers below too! This time each team has played 3 matches. Work out the numbers and enter them in the squares.

Team	Played	Won	Drawn	Lost
Orlando	3	2	1	0
Seattle	3		0	1
Kansas	3	1	1	
Minnesota	3	0	0	3

Enter your score for this page: ☐ — ☐

Check the boxes next to the shirt numbers which are multiples of **10**.

In the past, first team players wore only numbers 1 to 11. Nowadays some players wear really high numbers!

Enter your score for this page:

Check the box next to the shirt numbers which are multiples of **5**.

25 ☐   15 ☐

8 ☐   10 ☐

35 ☐   18 ☐

23 ☐   45 ☐

Numbers first started appearing on the back of soccer shirts in 1928

Enter your score for this page: ☐ — ☐

Puzzle time!   Look closely at the soccer field below…

How many rectangles are there in the picture?

If you answered the question correctly then enter a score of 1-0 here:

To give you an understanding of numbers in soccer, read out the following...

Typical number of goals scored by a team per match: 1

Typical team number for a striker: 10

League champions might score this many goals in a season: 100

Number of people at a lower division match: 1,000

How many dollars a player earns each week: 10,000

Number of spectators watching a cup final: 100,000

Amount of money to buy a player: 1,000,000

Amount of money to buy a good player: 10,000,000

Amount of money to buy a brilliant player: 100,000,000

How many did you say correctly? How many did you get wrong?
Enter your score for this page: ☐ — ☐

What part of a soccer ball is shown below? Is it a half (1/2), a quarter (1/4) or an eighth (1/8)? Write the answer as a fraction in the box…

Which one of the boxes below has the correct 4 quarters to make up a soccer ball.

Enter your score for this page:

It's Saturday afternoon. Soccer time!
Where the hands are missing on the clocks below – draw them in...

The soccer match kicks off at **3:00pm**

The first half lasts 45 minutes

The first half has finished at **3:45pm**.

Players have 15 minutes to eat their half-time oranges!

The second half begins at **4:00pm.**

The second half lasts 45 minutes

Full time! The match is over at **4:45pm.**

Enter your score for this page:

22

A **league** match is made up of 2 halves of 45 minutes each. How many minutes is that in total?

$$
\begin{array}{r}
45 \\
+\ 45 \\
\hline
\end{array}
$$

If a player is shown a red card by the referee then he is sent off!

If a player is shown one yellow card then he is in trouble but is not sent off.

From the team sheet below, how many of this team's players were left on the soccer field at the end of the match? [ ]

1.   Smith
2.   Jones
3.   Barrett
4.   Williams
5.   Holmes
6.   Moyo
7.   Robson
8.   Green
9.   Perch
10.   Davis
11.   Walker

Enter your score for this page: [ ] — [ ]

Below is a team sheet showing which players scored in a soccer match and how many goals they scored.

If you look at New York's team, then you can see that their number 8, "Francis" scored 2 goals.

Add up the number of goals each team scored and enter them in the boxes, to find out who won.

New York ☐ - ☐ Kansas

New York		Kansas	
1. Wilson		1. Gill	
2. Callaghan		2. Bibby	
3. Barnes	1	3. Skupski	
4. Nimz		4. Nicholson	
5. Hool		5. Carlisle	
6. Meek	1	6. Reeve	1
7. Marshall		7. Keegan	1
8. Francis	2	8. Goldstein	
9. Ray		9. Loberman	
10. Jackson	2	10. Stewart	1
11. Zaman		11. Haigh	

If you answered the question correctly then enter a score of 1-0 here:

If a **cup** match is a draw after 90 minutes then a further 30 minutes is played to see if one of the teams can win. How many minutes is that in total?

$$\begin{array}{r} 90 \\ +30 \\ \hline \end{array}$$

LOGIC PUZZLE!

A top league player wanted to wear the number 9 shirt when he joined a new club. But one of his new team mates already had that shirt number. The player therefore decided to choose the shirt number 45.

Can you think why he chose that number?

Hint: It is to do with adding two numbers to make 9.

Enter your score for this page: ☐ — ☐

Answers

Page

1) The team is playing in a **diamond** formation

2) 4

3) (a) Pentagon (b) Hexagon

4) 6,4,6,2,8,4,8,6,2,2,4

5) 1,5,7,5,9,3,5,3,9,3,9,7

6) (a) 18 (b) 4

7) (a) 12 (b) 12 (c) 24

8) ¼

9) 6,3,12,9,6,9,15,18,12,15

10) (a) 2 (b) 1

11) (a) +2 (b) +1 (c) 0 (d) 6

12) (a) 12,16, 20, 24 (b) 6

14) 7

15) (a) 2 (b) 2 (c) 2

16) (a) Houston have lost 1 match. Miami have won 0 matches.

    (b) Seattle have won 2 matches. Kansas have lost 1 match

17) 20, 30, 40, 50

18) 25, 35, 15, 10, 45

19) 7 (The field + The two halves + The two penalty areas + The two six yard boxes).

21) (a) ¼ (b) The second box is the correct one

23) (a) 90 (b) 9

24) New York 6 – 3 Kansas

25) (a) 120 (b) 4+5=9

Books by Adrian Lobley

Math

Book 1: The Soccer Math Book   (Age 4-6)

        El libro de matemáticas de fútbol (Spanish version)

Book 2: The Soccer Math Book   The Re-match! (Age 5-7)

Book 3: The Soccer Math Book   The Christmas Match (Age 6-8)

Book 4: The Soccer Math Book   The Birthday Party (Age 7-8)

Book 5: The Soccer Math Book   The World Cup (Age 9)

Reading

A Learn to Read Book: The Football Match   (Ages 4-5)
A Learn to Read Book: The Tennis Match   (Ages 4-5)

Historical Fiction

Kane and the Mystery of the Missing World Cup
Kane and the Christmas Football Adventure

Humor

The Ridiculous Adventures of Sidebottom and McPlop (Ages 7-10)
The Footballing Adventures of Sidebottom and McPlop (Ages 8-11)

For more information go to www.adrianlobley.com

Printed in Great Britain
by Amazon